THE FUN DEPT.®

Creating Opportunities for People to Have Fun at Work!

PLAYING IT
FORWARD

**Because *FUN MATTERS* for Employees,
Customers, and Bottom Line**

Nick Gianoulis & Nat Measley
THE FUN DEPT.®

ISBN 978-0-578-17387-0
The Fun Department, LLC
1813 Marsh Rd., Suite E Wilmington, DE 19810
(302) 731-8800
www.thefundept.com
create@thefundept.com

© 2015 by Nat Measley and Nick Gianoulis
Cover Design by Winning Edits
Book Design by Planet Ten
"The Fun Dept." logo is a trademark belonging to The Fun Department

Published and Printed in The United States of America

First I would like to acknowledge all of the entrepreneurs and visionaries out there who pursue their passion and dreams. I would like to acknowledge my partners (former and present); employees; interns; and customers for whom without our business would not have been possible; my daughters, Alexis, Ashley, and Alyssa who make my world complete; my mom; sisters; Debbie, Donna, and Diane; and best buds, Mark and Dean who have offered their constant support. Special acknowledgments and thanks to Jayla Boire, Jared Cohen, Ben LeRoy, Maria McCool, Brooke Miles, and Nat Measley who more than anyone is responsible for our success. I dedicate this book to you my friend.

-Nick

This work is dedicated to The Original Fun Dept. – Nick, Jayla, David, and Mark.

This work is dedicated to my family and friends; to my parents who knew I'd always end up working for The Fun Dept. – in some way – and to my sister who gave me some of my first fun department deliveries.

This work is dedicated to anyone out there in the world who has researched, attempted or considered fun for their organization. Keep up the good work!

-Nat

TABLE OF CONTENTS

FOREWORD

Who ever said work isn't supposed to be fun? Who created that silly belief? And why do we allow that belief to continue to perpetuate in our work environments? Who seriously wants to go into a boring, scary, toxic environment every day? I sure don't and I am sure you don't either. Having fun in the work place can actually help improve innovation, productivity, communication, collaboration and so much more, this is why I love the book that you are holding in your hands.

I believe we are all a lot more alike than we recognize. One thing I know we all have in common is our desire to be loved, accepted and happy. Anyone who denies that is lying to themselves to "be tough" to feel protected. That "protection" is only an illusion. So how have we gotten so far from what matters to us most in our expectations of life? It seems more people think life is about suffering than happiness. Too many people have bought into self-limiting, scarcity-minded beliefs that hold them back from actually living their potential.

Potential is the thing that most people have been lead to believe only occurs if you apply yourself in school. The better your grades the more you will actualize your potential. While I believe education is part of our actualization, I believe it is only one part. We are collectively missing the most important "parts" of what really helps us maximize our potential. I believe it is reached through many characteristics – empathy, compassion, authenticity, innovation, effective communication, vitality and clarity on our purpose – just to name a few.

Interestingly enough, we don't focus on the characteristics mentioned as a core competency in school, nor in "job training". Sadly, up until now, these skillsets have been called "soft skillsets", which meant they were believed to lack impact on the bottom line. However, they have recently been called "impact skillsets" because the world is finally recognizing the immense value these skills have. So what's the connection between these skills and the book you are about to read, you wonder?

This book will open up your mindset to see new perspectives. It will guide you to implement more productive rituals into your work life. And it will transform your environment to stimulate greater potential in all of your colleagues, especially if they are millennials or millennial-minded.

We are at the brink of a tipping point around leadership, where old, fear-based leaders who demand respect will quickly fall away, and enlightened leaders who empower others will rise quickly in their ability to impact. If you are reading this book, I am going to assume you are in the latter leadership group and this book will be a great resource for you, to guide the implementation on a culture that ignites growth and ingenuity. Because, it will remain very challenging to access potential from people if they are sitting in stark, sterile, serious, stressful environments on a daily basis.

I applaud the authors, Nick Gianoulis and Nat Measley, on their path to raising awareness around the definitions of success and what creates it, as well as you the reader, for having an open mind to continuous personal growth and cultural transformation.

− Jen Groover

Serial entrepreneur, author,
motivational speaker, TV host,
and UN Delegate

Author of <u>What If? & Why Not?</u>

HOW TO READ THIS BOOK

You bought this book and opened it. Great job! After all, 80% of success is showing up. You're interested in creating fun at work so that you will develop an engaged, loyal, productive, and motivated workforce. We are interested in helping you understand how to deliver it and reap the benefits of fun at work by sharing our experience.

You will achieve insight from this book regardless of how you read it, but we ask you to consider two directions. First, read the book in the order it's written. Each chapter is progressive. When you reach the end of the book, you'll have the foundation, approach, and measures necessary to envision your very own fun department. And you'll know why it's important to your business' bottom line.

Second, keep in mind that the book is co-authored. You'll get real world scenarios from our founder, Nick Gianoulis, and practical application, stats and mechanics from our CEO Nat Measley. Put it all together and you've got context, background, and organizational development insights you won't find anywhere else on the planet. So don't skip ahead! You might miss a critical step in your mission to build fun into the fabric of your workplace culture.

Preface

The Fun Dept. gathered up a decade of our work, notes, and observations and put it here to give you a unique perspective and thorough understanding of fun in the workplace and how it can influence your culture and your bottom line in a positive way. It has always been our mission to create opportunities for people to have fun at work. Now we want to "play it forward".

We take fun seriously – because we've witnessed first-hand the impact it has on workplace health, productivity, relationships, loyalty, and motivation (and that's the short list of benefits).

We've developed a universal model we hope to teach you. We want to help you create a culture of fun at work. Our goal is to guide you to develop the vision and structure for not just a fun-filled office – but to get you started in the development of a "fun department" that stays on the org chart for good. We want to help you realize the many rewards our customers (from Fortune 100 companies to small, regional superstars) have enjoyed as a result of following The Fun Dept. model – with our support and services – providing team building, corporate culture shifting events, and long-lasting employee engagement.

Whether you're a CEO, HR executive or department leader, you know the value of employee engagement. But how do you get your employees engaged and keep them that way?

Nick Here...

I can relate to the anxiety this question can cause. For a couple decades – before launching The Fun Dept., I worked as a sales executive at an 80-million-dollar product distribution company, investing ample financial and human resources in employee engagement. I was also an active participant of the company's "fun" team, a group of creative people who committed to monthly planning and brainstorming together to stage the next big idea for those always-exciting employee events.

The committee cost the company money; not just cash but valuable employee production time. Further, no one on our committee was an employee motivation expert – and our team members were often stumped in our search for the next creative idea that would prove fruitful to motivate and engage our various and diverse colleagues – from warehouse staff and drivers to the CFO and receptionist. And we always had to justify our budget; our time and out-of-pocket costs, to management.

As luck and fate would have it, and along life's superhighway of serendipitous events, I gained a reputation for being "fun". When I'd arrive at a social gathering, I'd be greeted with some new twist on this exclamation: "Let the games begin! The Fun Dept. is here!" Admittedly, I was "that kind of person," gregarious (I was in sales), happy, and enthusiastic about the simplest of things —good friends, loving family, and a healthy life. I'd often get to talking – and dreaming – about having an actual fun department at work. I'd always agreed that a life at work where there was a fun department on the org chart would make for some very (very) good days at the office.

Frustrated with the daily grind and looking for an entrepreneurial outlet, I finally sat down with the original partners of what is now The Fun Dept. and translated the jumble of ideas about this new business model into a CEO-appropriate conversation, and took the "show" on the road, so to speak with a few early, closely connected corporate clients.

And you know what our team heard when we sat down with chief executives and human resources experts, every time the rough concept of fun at work was presented? Universally the general response was: "Can you help us right now? We're all out of ideas!" Or: "This never gets done – the fun. If you would do this for me right now I'd pay you whatever it takes." Or: "This is exactly what we need. Right now." We were excited after the first positive feedback on our fledgling idea. But we needed measurable and valid substantiation for the concept's outcomes before we could hit up the Fortune 100. Knowing anecdotally, through personal experience, that fun at work made good business sense, we set out to find proof for its impact on the bottom line. We met with Dr. Paul McGhee, a highly-regarded authority in the field of fun at work and operator behind www.laughterremedy.com.

Fortuitously, Dr. McGhee was right in our backyard in the greater Philadelphia region, and a 15-minute "Can-I-pick-your-brain?" session lasted hours. Dr. Paul McGhee was an authorized trainer and speaker for FISH!, a popular concept (and book) about the process and outcomes derived from creating fun for a fishmonger gang in Seattle. Dr. McGhee would spread the word – and philosophy – based on the book's principles and details. And he would deliver the message that fun at work is important. Yet, as we learned in the discussion and original presentation of The Fun Dept. concept – our concept and offering was unique because we were all set to actually structure, develop, and deliver the fun at work. Dr. McGhee didn't teach people how to deliver the fun (they weren't about to toss whole fish to one another in the conference room at work). "This approach offers companies the missing link," Dr. McGhee said in that first meeting. "You can deliver the fun. You're the tail of the FISH!" he said.

We got critical encouragement, measures, and a library of books from Dr. McGhee that day. And the next thing I knew, I had quit my job, and our original partnership had finalized a business plan, and we were building the infrastructure for delivering fun at work. The Fun Dept. was born. It was heady stuff. And those friends, the ones who called me "the fun department?" I think they changed my moniker from "fun" to "crazy" – leaving traditional corporate work behind to create a company that delivered fun at work seemed a little risky.

Before we could begin to deliver the fun, we needed a delivery team. At launch, we were calling these people "Funsters" for lack of a better term, and were looking for creative, dramatic, organizationally dynamic people. We had an idea to help us find the right fit; as a result of a recent consulting gig, we'd reconnected with an old friend, David Raymond. David was the first ever Phillie Phanatic, the boisterously recognizable team mascot for the Philadelphia Phillies baseball team. He transformed mascot entertainment, was a world renowned leader in the sports entertainment industry, and was recognized by Forbes magazine as the best mascot of all time. A light bulb moment occurred as we were discussing how to deliver engaging, stylized programs to corporations; this prompted our team to suggest we meet with David to explore his ideas about how to deliver fun to the masses. As a performer, organizer, and entertainer focused on fun; there was no better resource for delivery. So we arranged a meeting to see what he had to say about The Fun Dept. idea.

Within days, we were gathered around a table presenting the concept to David Raymond and his production manager, Mark Doughty.

And within hours of that first meeting, we had started drawing up the agreement that would become the backing for our very own business – The Fun Dept. after the first positive feedback on our fledgling idea.

Our vision was becoming a reality! We were all absolutely over the moon; and after that first meeting among our team, I remember feeling exhilarated. I was shaking with excitement on the way home. Any doubts and fears were melting away, the closer we got to acting on our plans. How could we not do this?

The Fun Dept. officially launched in January 2005, with an event that introduced a small group of corporate guests to fledgling service plans at an intimate, yet powerful event. We presented our executive team: the Godfather of Fun (me, Nick), the Marketing Maven (Jayla Boire), the Lord of the Deal (Mark Doughty), and the Emperor of Fun and Games (David Raymond). We closed our first deal as a result of that party; it was a happy time. It was also time to get to work on delivering our product.

In those first few years, the economy was doing fine; most companies were focused on attraction and retention, all competing in the "talent wars". And we were working with companies of all types and sizes. Our understanding that fun at work is a one-size-fits-all kind of business would quickly be vetted in the marketplace. Whether we were working with the global pharmaceutical company or one of the largest convenience store chains in the country, or the local plumbing and heating service leader – everyone was reaping the financial and retention, recruitment, and morale-boosting benefits of engaged employees. I'm proud to say that we were fortunate to be working with great people from Astra Zeneca, QVC, ING Direct, W. L. Gore, Vanguard, and Johnson and Johnson just to name a few. And this doesn't mean that we weren't working with small and mid-sized businesses, too.

Within the first year, we'd met and hired dozens of "Team Fun" Members, including Nat Measley, now one of the company's Managing Partners and my co-author for this book. Nat's innate talent, facilitating engaging fun in an inclusive and enthusiastic style, his grad school reasearch in Organizational Development, and his leadership skills would quickly make him a rising star in client and delivery management. And that's

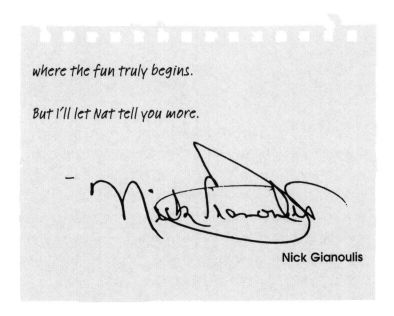

where the fun truly begins.

But I'll let Nat tell you more.

Nick Gianoulis

Nat here...

When I met Nick and David Raymond, in that first year that The Fun Dept. partners were busy launching the business, I was working for a national sport management company. My employer managed a minor league baseball team just north of Baltimore in Maryland. The organization was highly successful. They embraced fun as part of their culture, and integrated fun into the company's work product; fun presented in the game of minor league baseball.

This specific group was among the first sport management companies to sell out their 7,000-plus seat baseball stadium every night for the first five years in business. And that is because the team's management worked diligently to engage and entertain fans. And keep them engaged, entertained, and coming back for more.

As sponsorship manager, game entertainment coordinator, and on-field emcee, my responsibilities were diverse, but they always included personal delivery of crowd entertainment. As I was cheering up the crowd and performing some entertaining antics on top of a dugout, Nick and David were watching and saw one-third of my job responsibilities (but maybe the most important part at the time). Little did they know, and happy they were, to learn that the rest of my work was helping sponsors invest in fun at the baseball games – and making those investments memorable and engaging by using entertainment to deliver lasting, meaningful sponsor messaging. After all, the best way to promote our sponsors was to make their message truly memorable.

I did not realize it at the time, but my delivery model for fun at our minor league baseball venue – a combination of strategic customer insight, fun delivery, and engaging public speaking – would contribute significantly to the successful evolution of The Fun Dept. model.

On completion of grad school (University of Delaware, MPA focused on Organizational Leadership), I was fortunate to entertain two job offers: one as a sports management director at a large university, and one at The Fun Dept. – to dive into their operation during their first summer up and running. The decision was tough, and ultimately I chose to provide workplace leadership and impact by incorporating fun into corporate culture, and I've never looked back. And as you read on, you will see why. But for now, here is Nick again.

Nat Measley

Ten years after launch, The Fun Dept. is much more than the fun delivery team we built when we started. Now, we empower companies to create their own fun. The evolved model, built on our decade of experiences and thousands of delivered programs is equally educational and consultative.

Along with workshops and consulting, The Fun Dept. expands and leverages the success of our colleagues, and those who carried the light to show the way to fun. We must certainly pay homage to the FISH! Philosophy. But there are also others from whom we've learned along the way: The Levity Effect by Adrian Gostick and Scott Christopher; Laughter and Learning: An Alternative to Shut Up and Listen by Peter M. Jonas; and Fun is Good by Mike Veeck. And without that first fateful hours-long meeting and enthusiastic support of Dr. Paul McGhee of The Laughter Remedy, who knows if we would have ever gotten our company off the ground.

And now we are pleased to teach you "how to" actually do it.

Welcome to results-driven employee engagement, loyalty development and productivity growth - the world of workplace fun!

And again, I'll let Nat take it from here. But, I will pop

in from time to time with some of my notes, thoughts, and stories along the way.

PART 1

LET'S TALK ABOUT FUN AT WORK

CHAPTER 1

FUN IS SERIOUS BUSINESS: KNOW THY CULTURE, KNOW THY PEOPLE

"It is a happy talent to know how to play."
−RALPH WALDO EMERSON

When the Fun Dept. launched in 2005, the company was already keenly aware of the impact of workplace levity. And it didn't take us long to understand the serious impact of our work on employee loyalty, engagement, and motivation. Among our first appointments in the banking industry (here in Delaware there's a financial institution on every corner thanks to our legislative environment), we witnessed the differences firsthand. First we visited an up-and-coming online bank where the average employee was below 35 years of age, and enjoyed a culture rich with fun, creativity and teamwork – supported by an active and youthful HR department. That same day, we had the good fortune to also gain audience with one of the oldest financial institutions in the country, a bank founded by the prestigious capitalists who nearly single-handedly built the infrastructure for our surrounding area – the DuPont family. The cultural differences between the young, up-start and the Wilmington-based, historic, classic trust company were palpable. Not because one bank was "better" than the other, but because the work environments had developed and adapted according to the founders' orientation to business at the time they opened the doors, And it was quickly apparent to us, in meeting with leadership in both banks, why one was attracting and retaining the top talent in the country, and growing rapidly, while one seemed to be more stagnant in terms of growth and employee engagement. These first conversations quickly confirmed our research and development of our fun-at-work concept; fun makes a difference in the bottom line in more ways than one.

Have you ever walked into a business and immediately sensed if it was a good place to work? Have you ever said to yourself, "I'd love to work here" or "I'm not sure I would fit in here?"

The culture and environment of your office, and their contribution to employee happiness can have a major impact on your bottom line. In human resources, one very popular metric is employee engagement. It measures employees' emotional and active commitment to the success of the company. Engaged workers are enthusiastic about their jobs. They're dedicated to helping the company reach its goals. And disengaged workers? Not so much. They complain, make excuses, undermine others, and basically show up for work to collect a paycheck. According to a Gallup® survey [1], a company loses $2,246 per disengaged employee per year. Why? Disengaged employees take more sick days. They arrive late more often. They miss deadlines. They're more likely to instigate customer complaints. In all, they drag people down. They drag business down.

Engagement also impacts sales. According to PeopleMetrics', highly engaged teams sell over 20% more than poorly engaged teams [2].

---

1 "Employee Engagement: What's Your Engagement Ratio?" Gallup', 2008-2011

2 "Calculating the Cost of Employee Disengagement," June 13, 2011, PeopleMetrics'

And engagement affects turnover. Obviously, disengaged employees – no matter how talented they may be – are likely to quit. The more time and money are needed to train new employees. Now ask yourself: Are your employees engaged or disengaged?

As a leader, you'll never manage the emotional assets of every employee. But you can control how much you promote a positive culture in your workplace – one that encourages significantly higher levels of engagement through the time, talent, and dollars you invest in their engagement.

Fun (at least workplace fun) is not about hopping on one foot blindfolded, wearing embarrassing costumes, or forcing employees to be silly. Fun at work is building solidarity, connection, and an outlet for workplace stress. When designed and delivered at regular intervals with forethought and understanding about what your staff needs, fun at work will:

- Defeat burnout and boredom

- Enhance creativity and productivity

- Create energy, enthusiasm, and excitement

- Improve employee retention and prevent costly turnover

- Attract and retain the best staff

- Boost profitability

Check out one of our favorite books, The Levity Effect by Adrian Gostick and Scott Christopher for more data about the effects of fun on workplace engagement. One of our most motivating statistics in the early years was this: Among companies denoted as "great" in Fortune's "100 Best Companies to Work For" a whopping 81% of employees say they work in a "fun" environment.

Or – for more personal evidence – think back to your elementary school days. What was your favorite part of the school day? Remember recess?

Schools had recess for a reason, and it wasn't merely to give teachers a break from classroom time. According to the American Academy of Pediatrics, "well-supervised recess offers cognitive, social, emotional and physical benefits that may not be fully appreciated when a decision is made to diminish it." [1]. There's much substantiation among educational organizations regarding the benefits of recess and its importance to a child's development.

Sadly, now that we're grown up, we have set aside our need to play; in fact, you might even say we've forgotten how to play. We no longer enjoy recess every day. Instead, we might just get it once a year at, say, the company picnic. Then "recess" just seems awkward, right? (Do you find it odd to see your coworkers in T-shirts and jeans?) Many folks feel much more at home in their cube nest, protected from observation by six-foot partitions, glued to their desks, staring at their monitors, at least eight hours a day, five days a week.

Some jobs seem even worse. Look at fishmongers. Imagine that your job is to stumble out of bed in the wee hours of the morning to filet fish to sell to the masses. But the now-famous creators of the Fish! Philosophy, those fishmongers in Seattle, prove it's possible to transform any work environment into a place of fun. At the Pike Place Fish Market, employees toss fish in the air. They engage passerby in their antics, catcalls and performance art... and subsequently sell boatloads of fish - pun intended. And they have transformed their smelly fish stand into a tourist destination. In fact,

---

1 "The Critical Role of Recess in School," Pediatrics®, December 31, 2012

their story inspired the book: <u>Fish! A Remarkable Way to Boost Morale and Improve Results</u> by Stephen C. Lundin, Harry Paul, and John Christensen.

The Fun Dept. picks up where the FISH! Philosophy leaves off, describing not only the "why" of fun, but also the "how to" of fun. We show you how to welcome recess back into your day. We teach you how to design and develop custom programming that harmonizes with the personality and culture of your workplace. There's no one-size-fits-all with fun.

So, whether you manage a fish stand or a financial institution, fun can be an integral part of your workplace. But where do you start? How do you get your team to embrace a new mindset of fun? It all begins with leadership. Read on as we illustrate examples of how leaders embraced workplace engagement and fun, with measurable results.

CHAPTER 2

LEADERSHIP:
IT ALL STARTS AT THE TOP

Are you thinking that fun at work sounds really good? And are you beginning to understand the potential and impact of developing an engaged employee culture? Close on the heels of your light bulb moment, you're probably wondering what you could possibly do to a) get your management on board with the notion or b) persuade your management colleagues to examine the potential. Because fun-at-work is often viewed as a time-management (or mismanagement) issue, some leaders think of fun as a three-letter "f" word. If employees are having fun, they're not spending time being productive. They're away from their desks – missing phone calls, emails, meetings, and more. We consider, frankly, only the opportunity costs.

Conversely, employees may consider fun at work a waste of valuable career-building time, even a possible threat to their upward movement at work. Only "slackers" have fun, right? We're recognized for accomplishment. If an employee is caught goofing off, they could be viewed unfavorably by management; denied raises or promotions or advancement. Who wants that?

That's why we have always pitched the concept of employee engagement and fun at work to the most senior level management team with whom we could get time on the calendar. If leadership isn't leading the charge, employees will hesitate to engage, and that will undermine the initiative from before the first fun idea leaves the planning group and makes its way into the office. Leaders launch the fun; informing employees not only that it's OK to have fun, but that they are going to be right there with them. When it comes to fun – or any major organizational initiative, leadership support is key to success and impact.

So what challenges, roadblocks, and objections might you face when you are considering the development of employee culture through fun at work? Let's tackle the most common objections we've seen in our experience in program development. They may be your own concerns, or the concerns of other leaders in your organization – in any case, prepare for naysayers with our help. If you are petitioning for leaders' support, use the information here and in the referenced chapters to make the business case for fun and answer the hardest question. How can a leader say "yes" to fun without sacrificing their business?

FUN MYTHS TO DEBUNK RIGHT NOW

#1 – Creating fun is expensive and time-consuming.

The typical model for fun is the company holiday party at a large banquet hall, or some fast-paced, one-and-done, day of teambuilding that replicates the popular "Survivor" series on television. The time and money invested on these kinds of events, along with the stress of planning, organizing, and ensuring participation company-wide, can make fun, well … unfun. And, though these events offer great opportunities for teams to connect, we agree, they can become quite costly.

In Chapter 5, we will show you how the least time-consuming, stress-free, and regularly scheduled (even virtual) acts of fun can make a positive impact and bring measurable results. Our tried-and-true process and practice will reform your view of fun at work. Through cost-effective, brief, and well-designed deliveries of fun, delivered to small groups over time, your company will develop a customized model that is seamless and stress-free in form and function. And, you'll find that short, regular engagement produces longer-term results. The notion that fun is expensive and time-consuming comes from the historic delivery of fun you get twice a year – at the holiday party and the company picnic. We want fun to be efficient and effective!

#2 – Fun is frivolous.

Well, this objection has an easy answer and it's all in the dollars and sense. Remember our quote from Gallup*? Companies lose an average of $2,246 per disengaged employee per year. Can you do the quick math and determine what that might mean to your bottom line? Increasing employee engagement is anything but frivolous.

When fun is implemented strategically, it can have serious benefits and impact. It can boost productivity. It can promote health and happiness, enhancing employees' morale and creative spirit. And isn't that what we want for employees – for them to be happy, healthy, productive and bursting with creativity?

#3 – Employees don't want to make fools of themselves; they won't want to participate.

Yup, being self-conscious among co-workers can be a barrier. We've seen it in action. Most people are self-conscious to some degree. When leadership is aware of the existing personalities and culture, and planning thoughtfully to get everyone involved in an employee-focused event, you will prepare for those uncomfortable few who may work to be wallflowers.

Through deliberate planning, and with experience (and a little help from The Fun Dept.), trust and optimism will win the day – and you'll master the art of engaging even the most shy among your colleagues.

#4 – I don't want to deal with the office politics that might crop up.

Office politics, hierarchy and trust issues affect every workforce. You might wonder what would happen if you brought all of that unrest and buried feelings into an enclosed space for a "fun" event. Would that simmering pot boil over?

Nah, we can assure you, after watching the fun in real life everything irons out once the right programs are in place. With years of fun under our belts, we have witnessed more unity than disconnection, and a surprising breakdown of barriers and dissolving of politics. Turns out that fun programs – when done right – actually serve to bond your staff together. Office politics and drama take a back seat to fun. Employees want and need to bond and see each other in a new light. Give them that chance, and you'll see it for yourself.

#5 – I am not sure I know how to create fun that my staff will enjoy.

We can relate. When The Fun Dept. launched, we studied, researched, and developed hundreds of sustainable and easily adopted engagements that had broad appeal. We know that committees and clubs and any number of groups are put together (and eventually fall apart) to come up with ideas.

Sharing the brainstorm process is what we do. In Chapter 7, we'll show you a handy technique for generating hundreds of ideas for employee engagement and fun programs!

#6 – I don't feel comfortable promoting fun (and I don't feel like I'm the most fun person, either).

Relating to your staff, employees or workforce isn't always a natural or innate talent, that's true. We are culturally developed in ways that are specific to our work environment, upbringing, or beliefs and values. Leadership in employee engagement begins with taking responsibility for the uptick in morale, productivity, and creativity.

Just because the development of an engaging culture – or fun at work – does not feel natural does not mean it can't happen; it simply means you need a launch plan and design support for your program, and (beyond this book) you may need a little hands-on help from the experts.

#7 – Getting expertise to help develop programs is expensive, right?

Okay. We have to spend some time on this objection.

We hear this worry for two reasons. First, few operational budgets include a line item for employee engagement. So fun is already breaking the budget. (Luckily, there's an easy solution: Add a line item. And then watch other line items improve!).

Second, most companies' leaders attempting to develop a fun culture with employee engagement throw a big wad of dough at the wall once and hope it "sticks." They usually spend more money than we would ever recommend. A great example of how a large investment can actually be wasted is the big, exciting "giveaway" – one of our clients actually provided an iPad™ to all employees. Thousands of dollars later, did employees really feel special? Was their experience truly memorable or personal? Were employees connected to the business or the giveaway? Remember the famous line from a song, an adage we often use in real time: "Money can't buy me love?" Well that's a truism. And where the one-and-done employee events are concerned (you know, the holiday party or employee picnic), well that is a substantial investment, too, with hidden opportunity costs our clients do not often consider. Account for the opportunity time and talent spent, as well as out of pocket expenditures. Some companies spend too much time in pre-party planning. (If you have been a part of an Employee Events Committee, raise your hand!). Here is a real-life example:

Number of Employees in Committee
10 (5% of total workforce)

Number of hours in committee meetings per month, per employee
Four

Number of hours additional committee planning and implementation per month, per employee
Two

Average employee hourly rate (including benefits)
$50

Cost per month
$3,000

These numbers don't even include the cost of party supplies, prizes (iPads, please!), and other props. Also missing are the opportunity costs – the work missed while employees are planning the events. And don't forget the cost of pizza to feed your team during event planning meetings. How else can you get people to volunteer?

We've developed models at The Fun Dept. that deliver just as much engagement, and employee fun – if not more – at a fraction of the cost. You will get details in Chapter 7. There really are cost-effective ways to lift everyone's spirits without breaking the bank.

ARE YOU WALKING THE TALK?

We've helped you overcome some objections about fun and eased your doubts. That's great! After all, fun in the workplace begins with you - the leader.

And just like it begins with you, it can also end with you. You have the power to support it or to squash it. Your actions are very important. If you are just paying lip service to engagement and fun, without actions to match, the initiative will fall flat.

For instance, let's say it's the day of a teambuilding event. It may be tempting to pull the ole' email-in-the-corner trick; that's where you announce to your staff – via email from your corner office – that the "fun" has begun. Everyone leaves their workspace but you. You are still doing your normal job ... and emailing in the corner. Or, you show up to the activity and stand in the corner of the room, with your back turned as you answer emails with your thumbs.

From our experience, employees generally have a strong and accurate sense about whether their leadership cares or not. Show your employees that you care – that you're truly part of the team – by joining them in their new, fun adventures. That means:

- *Participating in the fun activities*

- *Being authentic in your participation*

But don't worry. We are not asking you to stand on a table, don a hula skirt, and belt out Jimmy Buffett songs til everyone laughs at (not with) you. You do not need to be the center of attention. You just need to be present, both physically and emotionally. As you will see in Chapter 5, you can be part of the fun in your own way and we promise it will not be another one of those "fun programs" that has everyone – especially you – checking your watch anxiously awaiting your return to work.

FUN IS NOT FOR ME? LEADERSHIP IN ACTION

A client in the home services business holds monthly meetings to recognize top performers. Each meeting kicks off with a brief icebreaker game or challenge, facilitated by the HR Director.

During the first few gatherings, the President would grab a cup of coffee and stand on the sidelines observing. He beamed his approval, but he did not participate. And no matter how hard the HR Director tried to persuade the President to join in, he abstained, citing his concern that he wouldn't be taken seriously as a leader. "My uncle, who founded this company, never played along," he said. "I want to let them know I'm happy for them, but keep my distance to keep their respect."

He set an example, by default. Soon, a VP and Director of Sales joined him to watch the action. (This is typical. From our experience, non-participation among leaders can be viral.)

When The Fun Dept. engaged the company as a client, we surveyed the employees about the icebreakers. The response was negative. Eighty-five percent of the workforce said that the fun felt forced and trivial. We received feedback such as: "The events are a waste of time." And: "Fun can't be all that important if my boss isn't part of it." (Their response is also typical; employees often complain that their "managers don't play.") Imagine the success of the icebreakers if the leaders put down that cup of coffee and stepped into the fun!

So, we challenged the company's leadership. We told them that they had good intentions, but their execution was failing. If they really wanted to change things for the better, they had to participate. No ifs, ands or buts. We give them a lot of credit, because they really listened to their staff and to us, and jumped in and played along. In a follow-up survey, 75 percent of the skeptical employees changed their minds. They now enjoyed the time together, participated fully, and embraced the fun. After all, the leaders got to know the employees, and employees got to know the leaders. Everyone bonded. The fun was meaningful and led to authentic team building within the organization.

See leaders? It's not that hard. All you have to do is play along (and really mean it).

CHAPTER 3

THE EVOLUTION OF FUN

Workplace fun is just like a fine romance. It starts with curiosity and attraction (yes, we want to have fun together and get to know each other better!). Then there are the "dates" - unique experiences and getting to know each other in a casual, appropriate setting. The company then starts scheduling fun programs at regular intervals. Finally, there's true commitment and long term engagement. The proposal to develop corporate culture and engage employees is answered with an "I do". Fun becomes an integral part of the corporate culture.

But even the best teambuilding venture – as romantic love, or any relationship – has its ups and downs. That is the human reality. We remind you about the reality because we do not want to encourage adoption of The Fun Dept. model in a way that sets up a belief that employee engagement and the many other benefits that a business receives adopting the model will happen quickly. Nor can the leadership revert to a set-it-and-forget-it program. Yes, we'll give you the benefit of what we have learned. We will support design and implementation of a customized program for your business. Essentially, we can give you all the tools for success. But prepare yourself for unexpected hurdles. It might be that Eeyore-like coworker whose gloomy utterances drag everyone down. Or that one teambuilding event that doesn't quite go as planned. As with any investment in human resources, an employee engagement program will require that you persevere through your challenges. Consider them learning, or research and development, experiences. Allow yourself, your company and your relationships to grow as a result of the lessons learned. As fun evolves so too can you.

Just as romantic or friends' relationships develop and change, so will your customized fun department. For instance, we know companies that, 10 years ago, spent more than $100,000 on employee events. But then the economy crashed. Thousands of people were laid off. The "lucky" employees who still had jobs endured; working harder and doing more than they had in the past. Morale plummeted. Companies – adapting to this new economy – had to find new and creative ways to rebuild team spirit, provide motivation, and reduce stress. And leadership had to do this without appearing condescending and inauthentic. Through early adoption of The Fun Dept. Model, our clients found that planning, implementation, and commitment created an adaptive, productive, and less-stressed workforce. While the economic environment may change, the model for delivering what employees need will not. They learned that brief, consistent, and cost-effective engagement will overcome even the most challenging business environment, and bring employees joy, stress reduction, and a willingness to persevere through difficult times at work.

Investment is key; advancements, engagement, stress reduction doesn't happen overnight. You will not be guaranteed immediate results, however, we can assure you after bearing witness to thousands of employees' experiences – your effort will pay off. But think of your program for developing fun events and employee engagement at work as a process, not a singular event. The program will evolve like every other aspect of your business.

Sometimes, just as in relationships, you might need to spice things up! Teambuilding programs can occasionally fall into a rut. A telltale sign is attendance. Are fewer employees coming to your events than before? If so, it may be that your workforce is changing while your fun programs are staying the same. Suppose you have a team of 10 people, and two are replaced. That's a 20% change! Unless the two newbies possess the same DNA and brain cells as their predecessors, your workplace dynamics will shift. The culture will shift, too. So the fun should shift as well.

In the next chapter, we describe fun as a shared experience. Your fun programs can be designed to have mass appeal. Solicit ideas from all employees about what they consider fun. And refresh your list often. We cannot emphasize this enough.

FROM BEER TO BABIES

As mentioned earlier, I spent a couple decades working for a large product distribution company – United Electric, a company that took fun very seriously. Sure, we had the traditional, annual summer picnics and holiday weekend parties. But most of our fun – especially in the company's earlier years – was impromptu and usually involved lots of food and drink. For instance, our new-employee orientations often included extended lunches and sometimes the rest of the day off! And on one memorable occasion, buses arrived late in the day to whisk all the employees to a surprise crab and beer celebration.

As fun as our fun was, the company had a "work hard, play hard" mentality that treated work and play as separate items. Work was on work time, and play was after hours.

Fortunately, as United grew and evolved, so did its fun. Eventually the company launched its own so-called fun department – the Circuit Club. I was an active member and even co-chaired the club for two years. As you will see, the club started with some "work hard, play hard" teambuilding and evolved into something a whole lot more mature. The key to our success: We gave ourselves permission to change.

Let's look at 20 years of the Circuit Club's highly fun evolution:

YEARS 1–5: KEG PARTY IN THE WAREHOUSE

When the Circuit Club first launched, we encouraged employees to share ideas for fun events and initiatives. We brainstormed a list of ideas, including:

- Close the shop early once a month and hold keg party in the warehouse

- Start meetings and trainings with "getting to know you" exercises

For the most part, our ideas focused on fun. And why not? Our employees wanted to connect with coworkers – as well as leaders – on a more personal level. Events like the monthly keg party fit the bill. Indeed, our "beer teambuilding" became a popular tradition. Cheers!

YEARS 6–10: EYES ON GROWTH

As the company evolved over the next five years, so did employees' priorities. Keep in mind that United was an employee-owned business. Employees had a vested interest in their professional growth and the company's success. We hired many new professionals to help us as we grew. Look at some of our ideas from this era:

- Conduct brief updates with incoming professionals and make them fun

- Offer unique training and development sessions on topics such as teambuilding, business management, ethics, creativity in the workplace, customer service and satisfaction, leadership, and employee engagement

- Start to research the outcomes of making every aspect of our business fun

We still embraced fun but defined it in a new way. Our new "fun" focused on business and professional development – and the celebration of our growing success. Like every other part of your business, fun evolves.

YEARS 11–20: TIME FOR FAMILY!

By now, the early days of the Circuit Club seemed like days of yore. Our employees had more on their minds than just post-work beers and professional education. They had diapers, car seats, daycare, school, homework, braces, after-school activities, and college savings to think of! That's right. Our employees now had kids.

Here were ideas from the moms and dads at United:

- Offer flexible work schedules and flextime reflected in hours and pay

- Provide resources to support families

- Further research the maturation of the fun and its cost

More and more, "fun" at United meant work-life balance. The Circuit Club's initiatives focused increasingly on ways to enhance family time and employees' overall wellbeing.

Does the story end there? No! From years 21 and beyond – as a new crop of employees joined United – our ideas list had a more cross-generational flavor. Seasoned employees collaborated with younger employees and shared their secrets for success.

The Circuit Club still exists and upholds United's mission for a happy, healthy workforce. And while the company has faced challenges – including a tough economy – its legacy of fun continues. And to think – it all started with some beer.

So fun is good and fun evolves. But, what is fun? And more specifically, what is workplace fun?

PART I: CONSIDERATIONS

Questions to Consider

• Leaders, which of our objections do you best relate to?
Do you have others? Why else would you NOT
endorse fun?

• Leaders, how are you perceived by your co-workers at
work? During fun programs?

• Have you seen fun evolve where you work? Why do you
think that happened?

• Has your culture changed as a result of fun program
evolution? How?

PART II

THE NEW RULES ABOUT FUN

CHAPTER 4

FUN IS A SHARED EXPERIENCE

"Laughter is an instant vacation."
-MILTON BERLE

Okay, we've provided some structure to help frame the experience of fun at work. Fun is good for business. Now, we really should define it. What exactly is "fun"? Everyone conjures up different images, activities, people, memories, and dreams when they think of fun. For you, fun might be picnicking and playing with your kids at the park. For your neighbor, fun might be curling up on the couch with a good book. For someone else, it's travel and adventure. For other folks, it may be so specific and personal that no one else can possibly relate.

So, when you're creating fun for a group where each person is unique, how do you pick the right activity?

I asked myself a similar question when I worked for the national sport management company. Part of my job was delivering on-field entertainment. That's right. Every sweltering summer night at the minor league stadium, my on-field promotions team and I delivered fun for 7,000 people. The fans' one common interest and passion, of course, was our team. But how else could I connect everyone in the ballpark?

What would everyone love? What would everyone get excited about? Eureka! It was the oldest trick in a minor league baseball entertainer's bag of tricks. I had seen it at other parks. We had done it every night at our stadium: the T-shirt toss. Every game, during the second inning, I'd grab the microphone and scream: "Are you having fun? Let's keep the fun going with some free T-shirts!" My crew and I (about 6 total team members) would burst onto the field and hurl as many as 100 T-shirts through the air. Some T-shirts were thrown with raw human power. Others were launched with a super-human cannon arm. We also used rubber slingshots and an official T-Shirt cannon – a compressed-air powered tube sitting on top of a trigger.

Shirts flew everywhere. People love winning. It's not about the free shirt; it's about the glory of victory. Fans would dive into another row of seats – and contort themselves as if playing Twister – to snatch the coveted prize. Even those who shied away from physical stunts loved watching the other fans go wild. Cheers filled the stadium. Mission accomplished.

Your task, as a leader, is to find the proverbial "T-shirt" that people will dive for.

To do this, let's take fun to a whole new, geeky level. Introducing – drum roll, please – The Fun Dept.'s handy *Fun For Me Listing Exercise*. You need at least two people to play. We've completed this exercise with as many as 2,000 in an auditorium. Set a timer for five minutes. When the clock starts, you and your buddies must each write a personal list of what you consider fun. That's right: five minutes to think, dream… and scribble furiously! Write down however many items you want. And there are no right answers. It could be spending quality family time or eating ice cream sundaes or playing air guitar to "Stairway to Heaven." (Did we mention this is a judgment-free zone?).

ARE YOU READY? GET SET...GO!
OH, AND NO PEEKING OR CHEATING.

TIME'S UP!

Take out another piece of paper. On it, draw interlinking circles – one circle for each participant. Who doesn't like a good, old-fashioned Venn diagram?

The diagram below is for two participants:

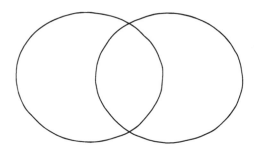

Next, put the names of each participant in each circle. Let's use Betty and Barb here.

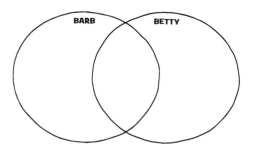

Next, share your *Fun For Me* lists. Enter items that apply only to you in the part of your circle that doesn't overlap other people's circles. And enter items in common into the areas where your circles cross over. For Betty and Barb, their circles might look like this:

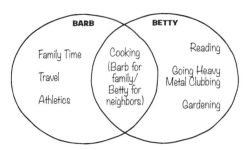

Who'd think a globetrotting family athlete would have anything in common with a Led Zeppelin fan? But it's true. In fact, every time we conduct the *FUN FOR ME LISTING EXERCISE* with two people – all around the world with folks of different ages and backgrounds – we find connections.

Not long ago, I completed this exercise with my dad, someone I've known my entire life. We found four common interests – two of which we didn't know about before! One newfound item was "singing in the car, loudly, with the windows up." Now, every time he visits me, I wonder if he jammed to Broadway show tunes on the way over. (Personally, I'd choose boy bands of the 90s.) Regardless of our music preferences, this exercise has strengthened our relationship. We realize we have even more in common, apart from height and mannerisms. In most cases, you are your father's son.

This brings us back to fun. Fun is where people's lists cross over. Fun is the "x." And "x" is what we define as a Shared Experience. **X = Fun = Shared Experience.**

Our model for fun comes from shared experiences. Shared experiences are precious. They help break down barriers. They're like the T-shirt toss, bonding 7,000 unique individuals in a minor league baseball stadium on a hot summer night.

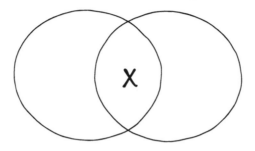

Now, let's do the exercise again. This time, the goal is to find the x/fun/shared experiences at your work. Like before, every answer is a good answer, but be sure to list only work-related items. Examples might be coffee breaks, brainstorming meetings, or throwing paper airplanes. Take five minutes to think.

GOOD LUCK...GO!
TIMES UP!

Was it harder to find common ground this time? It's easier to think of fun outside of work, isn't it?

An even bigger challenge is finding common ground among a larger group, like in your own office. Look at the diagram below.

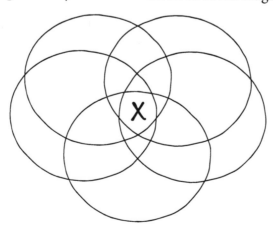

Even with just five employees – or circles – the opportunities for connection, upon first glance, decrease significantly. Or at least at first glance.

The key is repetition. The more often you perform this exercise, the more likely you'll find a connection among five people or even larger groups. (Remember: Every time we've done this exercise, we've found a match!) Also, even when you and your coworkers become seasoned veterans of fun, you should revisit your lists once and awhile. People change. Interests change. Life changes. The diagram is a living, breathing thing. So are your Fun For Me lists. Because, fun evolves.

In addition, keep in mind that people can enjoy the same "x" in different ways. Consider the *Fun for Me Listing Exercise* we recently conducted for a class of 50 college students studying leadership design. We asked two volunteers to jot down their lists, share their interests with the class, and hopefully uncover that "x."

Indeed, the two volunteers had one thing in common: cliff diving. That's right. Cliff diving.

We asked the other 48 students, "Who would NOT want to go cliff diving"? At least 20 students raised their hands. Then, we asked, "If we still chose a cliff-diving activity, like a competition, how would you want to participate?" Our goal was to find middle ground (for those who preferred staying on the ground). The 20 students came up with great ideas:

1. We can be the judges, scoring the dives from 1 to 10

2. We can be in charge of the food

3. We can take pictures and short videos and post them on social media.

One student said, "I'm a DJ. We can bring music and make introductions. As long as I'm not cliff diving, I'm happy!"

Brilliant, team! At first, students weren't sure how everyone could enjoy "x" – in this case, a scary activity like cliff diving. But with a little extra brainstorming, they uncovered ways to incorporate everyone's ideas of fun. If these students can make cliff diving fun for all, then you and your team can create tamer versions of fun, too! Yes you can.

TEAMBUILDING...WITH BODY ARMOR

Time for a quick break! Go google "booking.com paintball commercial", and watch the hilarious, 30-second video. It pokes fun at company retreats...and specifically event planners who choose a teambuilding activity that they alone consider fun. In this case, it's paintballing. As the other employees trudge around in body armor, they get killed by paint a million times over. Paintballing clearly wasn't on their Fun for Me lists! But there is happy ending. The deflated employees get to stay at a palatial, luxury resort...the "x" that incorporates everyone's idea for fun.

CHAPTER 5

THE 3C's: ESSENTIALS FOR HEALTHY, PRODUCTIVE WORKPLACE FUN

You know the ingredients: knowing your culture and your people, leadership, and investment. Now, let's look at the stage on which you'll perform the fun – or the healthy elements for the action.

A healthy program for fun at work has essentials, or foundations that ensure you will get the culture, leadership, and investment to perform optimally. We call them the Essential 3Cs.

The 3Cs are:

- *CONSISTENCY*

- *COMPANY TIME*

- *CULTURE COMPLIANCE*

Let's take a closer look at why consistency, and fun on company time, as well as compliance from your people, leadership, and cultural ambassadors will maximize the impact of fun at work.

CONSISTENCY

The traditional model for workplace fun generally involves two specific high-profile events. They give employees a chance to connect and share, celebrate, and bond. They're typically pure fun and have been around since the dawn of business. You probably already plan these events.

They are...
the Company Picnic and the Company Holiday Party.

You might spend months preparing for these celebrations. And they can be valuable for your team, no doubt. But any morale boost they produce is fleeting – maybe just a few days, or a week, tops. Before you know it, your employees may fall into a rut of apathy about the workplace; at least until the next special event many months later. Consider that this apathy, lack of motivation and connection costs you money. Productivity and loyalty are impacted.

That is why The Fun Dept. model is one based on a consistent delivery of engagement. When it comes to fun in the workplace, consistency is key. Fun should feel as natural and typical to the staff as the morning commute, coffee break, lunch, afternoon stretch, happy hour, and commute back home.

Our work and research has shown that most companies that offer fun on a more consistent basis have a workforce that's happier and more engaged.

Fun is like exercise. Stick to a consistent regimen, and you'll enjoy long-lasting results. So get out your calendar and a red pen, and select the dates for consistent fun. Don't know what activities to fill in on those select dates? Never fear. By the end of this book, you'll be a fun-generating machine!

FUN IN REAL LIFE – TIME AGAIN FOR THE COMPANY PICNIC

Charlotte is the Director of HR for a medium-sized life sciences company that produces and sells safety solutions to pharmaceutical distributors. Every year, Charlotte plans the company picnic. She arranges everything from the venue to the food to the fun. The annual event lasts for two hours on a weekday around lunchtime.

Without fail, for six months after the picnic and six months before the next one, the employees get restless. Where's the fun between picnics? And so, no surprise, engagement rates have plummeted over the past three years, based on survey results.

One of the company's competitors also holds an annual company picnic, organized by Arlene, the Director of HR. Arlene also plans picnics, but different ones. Hers are 30-minute lunchtime "mini-picnics," as she calls them, throughout the year. The events occur almost every month. Typically, excitement starts to build about two weeks before each mini-picnic, as employees look forward to the compelling fun, competition, and engagement – there is office "buzz" about teammate selection, strategy for winning, and reminiscing about the last event's winning moves.

Arlene's event enjoys 35 percent higher attendance rates than the events planned by Charlotte. And engagement rates have sustained or improved every year for the past three years, based on survey results. They're a better performing company. Big things can come out of little picnics!

COMPANY TIME

Studies conducted on employees and work-family balance show that employees value their time with family and friends much more today than ever before. Time is among the most highly valued "commodities." Yet, company leaders hesitate to schedule fun events on company time. Doing so, they believe, impacts productivity and is merely a distraction. Often, plans are made to usurp valuable down-time for employee engagement with events scheduled during evening hours or weekends.

Work is stressful enough. The gift of engagement in fun activities helps employees blow off some steam and stress, and re-set their perspective of their colleagues and daily tasks. That is why, we believe that:

- *Fun should happen on company time – whistle while you work!*

- *Fun can take less than 15 minutes, and it should!*

We often get calls from frantic administrators planning their sales and executive meetings. They want to hire us for a three to four-hour "teambuilding" event. When we ask about their agenda, it's always the same: meetings from 8:30 to 4:00 and teambuilding from 4:00 to 7:00. What happens at 7:00, we ask? Happy hour and dinner, the admins respond. Hmmm … that doesn't sound like fun for anyone. The "fun" is too long and disrupts family time. In fact, most formal fun that we've observe that is longer than a structured 90-minutes is too long, too boring and NOT fun.

So we offer this scenario: a 15-minute icebreaker at 8:30 to set the tone for a productive day, followed by a brief team activity after lunch to reenergize the group for the rest of the day and overcome the dreaded food coma. "What do we do at 4:00?" the admins ask. Our reply: "Let your people go. Send them home for some downtime. Be a super-hero and save the company some money and points on that employee engagement score!"

Sure, if we had our way, we'd have fun all day – every day. But then work really wouldn't get done. Sales would plummet. Production lines would halt. The United States' Gross Domestic Product would bottom out. Because The Fun Dept. doesn't want to instigate a national or worldwide economic collapse, we strongly recommend you set time limits on your company-time fun. Later in this book, you'll see what great fun you can accomplish in 15 minutes or less.

It is also easier to start adopting a culture of fun and workplace results, when fun is delivered in short stints. This is not to say that we are against moderate-length or longer fun events. We simply recommend consistency as a desired function – in lieu of a few events with longer duration. Plus, if you mess up that Company Picnic aren't the implications greater than messing up that 15-minute "fun program"?

CULTURE COMPLIANCE

The last essential C – Compliance – may not seem difficult. After all, who doesn't want to have fun? Compliance speaks to more than just our typical view of the concept, or legalities. Compliant fun will:

- Integrate with your company's culture

- Encourage everyone to participate – in their own way

First, make sure you have a good sense of the likes, dislikes, tolerances, and intolerances of the folks who make up your organization. Remember the Venn diagram we drew earlier? You're aiming for the "x" where the common interests intersect. Too many "fun" programs are really just fun aimed at the one or two folks who planned the event. Is that really fun … effective... or fair?

Second, fun needs to appeal to extroverts and introverts alike. Some employees will gladly do the limbo; others will prefer watching (and the sadists will volunteer to lower the pole). Everyone should feel comfortable enough to play along in the way that suits their tastes. Let the fun be customized to each person.

Here's an eye-opening example. An organization recently hired us to deliver some fun at their holiday party. Before the event, a pair of HR directors warned us how their employees were not fun. "Good luck engaging our group," one cautioned. "They don't like having fun at all."

About 100 employees attended the party. The Fun Dept. held a raffle along with some small trivia challenges around the room. Everyone participated in different ways, depending on their interests. As we mingled, we found the employees to be extremely friendly and gracious. They were, dare we say it, "fun"!

From our perspective, the HR duo misunderstood their workforce. What's more, as we learned, most of their past "fun" events forced people to participate in awkward, uncomfortable ways. No wonder they saw frowns, rather than smiles, from employees!

Thankfully, we had the chance to collaborate with HR well beyond the holiday party. We showed them how employees can participate in teambuilding events in different ways. The HR team took our advice. Over time, they strengthened their bond with employees. And over time, they enjoyed higher attendance at events. Post-event surveys also showed increasingly positive results.

The key to success? Allow team members to define their own fun. Listen. And plan events that allow for a variety of different kinds of participation.

Collaborative Fun is the Drug of Choice

A large, multinational biopharmaceutical company, contracted The Fun Dept. to deliver a series of fun programs at its global headquarters.

One event of the series was to be a surprise for about 100 HR managers and employees. As participants entered the room, they did not know why they were there or what was in store. Looks of confusion turned to looks of dismay when the staff saw us, sporting our obnoxiously bright T-shirts emblazoned with The Fun Dept. logo. Would this be one of those creepy, weird, teambuilding activities? Ugh.

One skeptic was a woman named Sally. When she spotted us, she clutched her clipboard and backed up against the wall. "I'm afraid," she muttered. We assured her that everything would be OK.

We played a brief game with two teams competing. The game ended in a tie. A tie? In all our rehearsals, we never anticipated a tie! Luckily, we did not have to improvise a solution, because the participants did. They asked to break the tie with a dance-off, much to our surprise.

Now, The Fun Dept. would never have suggested a dance-off. We would have assumed that workplace dancing would be awkward, at the very least. But these pharmaceutical staffers wanted to face the music and dance!

The biggest surprise? Sally, who verbalized her fears as we got the crowd going, volunteered for the dance-off. Plus, she busted a move, as we like to say, with a cartwheel when the call came to halt the dance-off came. Her brave dance finale won the competition.

That dance-off was a validating experience for both The Fun Dept. team and the leaders who engaged us to deliver the experience to their group. Although there was fear, uncertainty, and doubt exhibited by attendees at first, the assessment of what kinds of fun would resonate with the group, and the conscientious encouragement and attitude created not just a compliant crowd but an enthusiastic and motivated participant pool. Sally did not have to dance. She did not have to do a cartwheel. She just chose to. And that changed everyone's experience of the fun – not just Sally's.

LET'S BRING IT ALL TOGETHER

A solid teambuilding program must be Consistent, on Company Time, and Compliant. You need all three for your teambuilding initiatives to work, especially in the long term. Bypassing one or two can put the "un" in "unfun."

For your viewing pleasure, we've developed a handy chart to show what a company looks like when any of the 3Cs are included or missing from its teambuilding program. Our info is based on our own data as well as case studies over the past decade.

Which company looks like yours? Are you:

No Fun?

Some Fun?

More Fun?

or BIG Fun?

Regardless, there are challenges with each and work to do, no matter how fun you think you are.

	Organiza-tion	Consis-tent	Company Time	Compli-ant	Challenges
BIG FUN	#1	✓	✓	✓	The company should regularly update its list of fun ideas
MORE FUN	#2	✓	✓	✗	Less trust in leadership and risk of employees getting in trouble
	#3	✓	✗	✓	Compromised work time or personal time
	#4	✗	✓	✓	Uncertainty as fun is not part of the cultural fabric
SOME FUN	#5	✓	✗	✗	Disconnect between the fun at work and the company's culture
	#6	✗	✓	✗	Disjointed waste of work time
	#7	✗	✗	✓	Disjointed waste of personal time
NO FUN	#8	✗	✗	✗	Total disregard for the entire workforce

ORGANIZATIONS EXPLAINED

BIG FUN

Organization #1 is awesome. In fact, they are BIG FUN. Leadership understands the value of fun and plays along. They also have fun written into their workdays in short, consistent doses. The company should continuously refresh their inventory of fun ideas to keep employees engaged.

More FUN

Organization #2 implements fun consistently and on company time. But there is a disconnection with individual preferences, company culture, and policies. Employees may be reprimanded if they are having fun without the boss's approval. Or employees might not "buy into" the fun dictated by those planning it.

Organization #3 has fun that's consistent and compliant. But the fun is delivered outside of company hours and can disrupt employees' work-life balance. (Or, the fun is delivered on company time but eats up too much of the workday.) Leaders need to place more value on their employees' personal time. They should also learn how short, fun breaks during company time (15 minutes or less) can deliver a huge impact.

Organization #4 sees the value of fun, but when does it happen? Employees don't understand why fun occurs the few times it does, what they did to deserve the fun, or what they didn't do to miss out on the fun. It's a workplace filled with uncertainty.

Some FUN

Organization #5 delivers fun consistently, but it's not compliant or on company time. This is the typical and often non-sustainable "work hard, play hard" model that many companies champion. We think it's bogus, because it implies you must finish your work before you can play. It may work. In fact, it did at United Electric with Nick's Circuit Club. It can work if the culture demands it but is willing to change as employee lives and priorities change. A potentially more sustainable mantra, we believe, is "whistle while you work"! The Seven Dwarfs had The Fun Dept. model all figured out. They whistled every day (Consistent), excluded no one (Compliant), and built in whistling as part of their operation (Company Time). Snow White had some pretty smart friends.

Organization #6 conducts fun on company time, but the fun is inconsistent and goes against policies and individual preferences.

Organization #7 may have leadership agreement and support, but without the consistency or respect of employees' time, any fun programming is seen as a waste of time.

NO FUN

Organization #8 is a bummer. Don't work there. Fortunately, in our experiences of delivering fun at work, we've never met an Organization #8. Most companies fall between #2 and #7 … that is, before they adopt The Fun Dept. model. But the 3Cs are just part of the program. Keep on reading! Next, you'll learn how to create sensory connections among your staff, and take your teambuilding and fun to #1.

CHAPTER 6

FUN TICKLES THE SENSES

In the last chapter, we talked about how the 3Cs are critical for developing an effective teambuilding program. Now, let's talk about the five senses. Sight, hearing, smell, touch, and taste – they are our connection to the outside world. Fun should strike an emotional chord by tantalizing all the senses. It should look good, sound good, feel good, smell good, and taste good.

The Fun Dept.'s expert in multisensory fun is David Raymond, one of our original partners in fun. In David's early career, he was dressed head-to-toe in green fur as the Phillie Phanatic, the beloved mascot of the Philadelphia Phillies. David has delivered "phantastic" fun at some of the most respected sporting venues around the world.

During a typical game, David's fun interludes usually lasted a couple minutes and featured exciting, baseball-themed music like "Put Me In, Coach." He also made great use of props and other visuals – dummies dressed up like opposing players or managers, T-shirt cannons, four-wheelers, Phanatic-sized costumes, and more. Of course, no one really smelled, felt, or tasted him (thank goodness), but his entertainment became as much a part of the experience as fans savored the fluffy, sugary webs of cotton candy, the salty crunch of roasted peanuts, and the tangy relish on juicy hotdogs.

As the original Phillie Phanatic, David won everyone's affection. And believe us, Phillies fans are tough. They're known to throw batteries at Santa Claus and beat up the Easter Bunny (or at least, legend has it). David worked hard to connect with his audience on numerous levels, including the five human senses.

That is a positive example. Now let's consider the negative. How do people respond to engaging fun events that offend the senses?

Take the real-life example of the Hump Day Challenge – a monthly teambuilding event held at a call center for a staff of 15. The event takes place just after lunch on the first Wednesday of the month. That's when call volumes are lowest, so it's an opportune time to bring everyone together. Ryan, the manager, crafted the Hump Day Challenge to build team spirit and encourage greater connections among employees.

But Wednesday is not only Hump Day. It's also Ryan's day to eat chili. Unbeknownst to Ryan, but obvious to the entire team, his "silent but deadly" emissions have become part of the Hump Day Challenge. Even worse, Ryan hosts the event in his office, where the fumes are trapped. The smell is a displeasing distraction … and the only real thing connecting the team.

Or take the example of Liz, the CEO of another organization. She's coordinated the annual picnic ever since the business launched 10 years ago. She schedules the picnic right after the July 4th holiday, so that employees can enjoy a day with coworkers after some time off.

Every year, Liz calls the local state park and reserves their favorite pavilion. It's the perfect size for the group and adjoins a beautiful hiking trail. She also hires a DJ to play energetic music.

So far, so good, right? The event looks good (state park), smells good (food), tastes good (food), and sounds good (music).

But it feels horrible. The company is located in the hottest climate in the south; for the past five years, the picnic has fallen on days with scorching temperatures and oppressive humidity. The picnic is also held during the hottest part of the day – the mid-afternoon. Every year, people complain. They are hot. They are sweaty. They are cranky.

They have also repeatedly asked Liz to change the time and date. But Liz wants to keep everything the same – a picnic goes hand-in-hand with July 4th, after all! If you were Liz, would you respect your employees' wishes?

Bottom line: use common sense when it comes to the senses. Your teambuilding events shouldn't just look good on paper; they should also respect your employees with the right sounds, tastes, feelings, and smells. Appeal to all the senses, and, just like the Phillie Phanatic, you can build a devoted fan club.

MUSIC TO YOUR EARS – OR NOT?

A few years ago, The Fun Dept. conducted an experiment with one of our clients, one of the fastest growing colleges in the country for the past 10-years, Wilmington University.

The university hosted an employee health and benefits fair to educate employees on health options and smart lifestyle choices. The event was set up like a trade show, with vendors exhibiting at booths and mingling with employees. We were one of the exhibitors. Because of the university's large number of employees, half of the employees were invited on day one, and half on day two. Each day lasted two hours.

The Fun Dept.'s experiment tested how music (or lack thereof) would affect employees' perception of the health fair. The university not only blessed the experiment but encouraged it. They were always seeking ways to enhance the "look and feel" of their events and improve their already stellar – and may we mention award winning – employees' experiences.

On day one, we filled the room with Michael Jackson tunes, some group dances like the Cupid Shuffle and Cha-Cha Slide, and other fun songs. Music wafted across the room and permeated the event. On day two, we played music in spurts. We supplied it for just 15 minutes at a time, with five-minute breaks in between. During those music-free interludes, the only sound was the hum of conversations.

The difference between the two days was undeniable.

Day one had a certain energy – employees and vendors were bobbing their heads, tapping their toes, lip-syncing, and sometimes even breaking out some subtle dance moves.

Day two was decidedly sterile. No head-bobbing, toe-tapping, or lip-syncing. And certainly no dance moves. Plus, the interaction between vendors and employees seemed much more formal.

The post-event results were also striking. Day one was rated as more informative than day two, even though employees saw the same booths, read the same brochures, and spoke with the same vendors on both days. So, music not only created a positive ambience, but it also helped employees learn more about healthful living – a major goal of the fair.

PART II: CONSIDERATIONS

Questions to Consider

• Have you ever connected with someone that, upon first glance or impression, you felt you would not?

• Have you been part of a fun event and not participated because you felt you didn't have a role? Or felt there wasn't something offered to you that could be fun? Did you attempt to create a role for yourself?

• Where does your organization fall on our continuum; No Fun, Some Fun, More Fun or Big Fun? What are mechanisms you can implement to move up the scale?

• Have you experienced events or programs that did not consider the senses?

PART III

PLAYING IT FORWARD: FUTURE FUN

CHAPTER 7

LET'S BRAINSTORM SOME FUN!

Got leadership interest and support? *Check.*

Know your employees' interests? *Check.*

Understand the 3Cs? *Check.*

Want to design "fun" so that it appeals to all senses? *Check.*

Now you're ready for the creative job in building your Fun Dept. model. Let's build what we call your very own Creative Inventory! When you're done with this step-by-step exercise, you'll easily have hundreds – seriously, hundreds – of activities ready to use in the office. We call this a Creative Inventory brainstorm. Don't worry. These steps are simple.

STEP 1 – REVISIT COMMON INTERESTS

Grab that short list of common interests – or shared experiences – you created from the Fun for Me Listing Exercise. Make sure your list includes activities your company already does for fun. For that matter, gather all the folks who helped you with the listing exercise. And for that matter, grab everyone in your company for 5-minutes and ask them what they do for fun. Heck, even do it via email. They can help you brainstorm ideas for these next few lists...

STEP 2 – IDENTIFY FORUMS FOR FUN

Write a list of potential FORUMS, or venues, for fun. A FORUM may be:

- *A physical location that can hold a fun activity, like a desk, cubicle, office, boardroom, restroom, break room, kitchen freezer – we've heard them all!*

- *An experiential location that can fit in some fun. Examples include a company picnic, holiday party, weekly pow-wow, financial update meeting, safety training, internship program, orientation, community event, and more.*

STEP 3 – IDENTIFY THEMES FOR FUN

THEMES can be absolutely anything. Ask employees to write down their favorites from past work meetings or parties. (It's often easiest to think of ideas that have been done before.) Over the years, we've witnessed many fun themes, from sports-related active fun to beach scenes and food parties. We have even created custom trivia and scavenger hunt games. For your fun themes, tap into the culture and the types of fun that are most relevant to your people; or just ask around to co-workers to help you get started with the brainstorming.

STEP 4 – IDENTIFY ACTIVITIES YOU CAN EASILY IMPLEMENT

Ask employees for ideas of games or ACTIVITIES. The activities should be inexpensive, easy to plan, and quick to implement

(15 minutes or less). As with themes above, it's often easiest to brainstorm ideas that have been done or seen in the past. They may be things you've done at work, family games, fun on your own time, parties, or any themed concept from your original Fun for Me List. Here are ideas to get you started:

- *Copier Hangman*

- *Lunch of the Day Challenge*

- *Mix-Matched Socks Day*

- *Straight Face Laugh-Off*

- *Label-Maker Olympics*

Here are other creative ACTIVITIES, with some explanation:

New Hires, New Rules, New Voices

In a new employee orientation, encourage new hires to speak up and make you read the office policies and procedures in any voice or genre they like – rodeo cowboy, romance novel, Australian surfer – anything!

Pie the Prez

Yes. This is where you throw a pie in the president's face. It's a great test of your leader's commitment to fun! (We'll share a real-life example of Pie the Prez later in this chapter.)

Tally Marks Game

Any time a coworker brings up a non-work-related topic they always seem to talk about, give them a tally mark. Examples include kids, pets, and their favorite sports team. At the end of a week or month, the winner is the person with the most tally marks. The prize can be anything from a $10 gift card to a trophy. Or, the glory of victory may be enough! It always is for us.

What Will Spencer Wear?

Pick the guy or gal in your office with the best sense of humor (let's say it's Spencer). Everyone else guesses what they think he will wear the next day. The winner is the one who most closely predicts Spencer's clothing categories (khakis, jeans, or slacks / tie or no tie / black shoes, brown shoes, or sandals). The winner gets a picture with Spencer!

My Favorite Quote

Encourage people to write their favorite inspirational quote on a board. There's a reason Benjamin Franklin invented dry erase! Ok, it might not have been him, but regardless, use dry erase boards to update your quotes every day, week, month, or year.

STEP 5 – IDENTIFY WAYS TO FOLLOW-UP

When you have fun, you want that fun to last as long as possible, right? FOLLOW-UP helps you do just that. The actual event might just be 15 minutes long, but you can capture those fun memories and let them resonate through the corporate hallways for days, weeks, and months to come. And, you can promote those 15-minutes leading up to the fun as well. Pictures and videos are especially great for FOLLOW-UP. We also love simple emails or messages that recap who won, what they won, and when the next "fun program" will happen.

STEP 6 – PUT IT ALL TOGETHER. SEE WHAT YOU GET!

Guess what? You now have your very own creative inventory. Based on your team's ideas, you can mix-and-match your FORUMS, THEMES, ACTIVITIES, and FOLLOW-UP to create incredible opportunities for fun.

It might look something like this.

Here is how this applies to a specific examples. For instance, you could have a Stress Less / Straight Face Laugh-Off (THEME/ ACTIVITY) at the water cooler (FORUM) followed by an email blast with a photo of the straight-faced winner (FOLLOW-UP).

Even if you have just five ideas in each category, that's 5 x 5 x 5 x 5 or 625 combinations of fun. That would last more than two years if you held an activity every day, Monday through Friday.

Chances are, you have even more ideas than that. Imagine the possibilities!

STEP 7 – GATHER YOUR ADVOCATES FOR FUN

When it comes to fun, the more the merrier! And we don't just mean the number of folks attending your fun events. We mean the number of team members helping you plan events and championing the mission for fun.

We'll discuss strategies for building your own fun department – your "Team Fun" – in the next chapter. But for now, know that every organization has the makings of a fun department. Every organization has employees who would love to be advocates for fun, if given the chance. You just need to make your fun department slightly more structured, somewhat more active, and a lot more vocal!

AWESOME FUN IN ACTION

Working with organizations of all types and sizes, we've witnessed lots of unique and memorable examples of workplace fun. We hope you're inspired by the ideas below! However, don't just copy-and-paste these examples into your own fun agenda. Remember that every workplace is unique. What may work for one organization may need tweaking for another. Think about your employees, leadership, and corporate culture, and consider how to adapt these programs just for you.

Pie the Leadership

We worked with a medium-sized ATM management company based in the Philadelphia region. They consistently host employee events, and one in particular "took the cake" – well, the pie. The company's FORUM for fun was a 30-minute, late-afternoon celebration with light refreshments.

For the month leading up to the event, the leadership team had challenged employees to get involved in the community. The company's THEME for fun was Community Involvement.

Every time an employee signed up to volunteer – whether for mentoring, donating, or supporting a community event or nonprofit – their name was put into a hat. At the end of the month, the organization had two hats. The first hat was filled with all the employees' names. The second hat was filled with the names of employees who had served as volunteers. With two hats "brimming" with names, the team hosted a Pie the Leaders event – the ACTIVITY.

A volunteer pulled a name from the first hat; the winner got the chance to throw a mini cream pie at John, a company leader. Then a volunteer pulled a name from the second hat; this winner could throw a giant cream pie in face of another leader! These winners safely and gently cream-pied their bosses!

Although Pie the Leaders was a one-time event, it inspired lots of employees to volunteer in their communities over the next few months. So the fun – and spirit of giving – carried on. Pie the Leaders was one of the most meaningful activities we've seen anywhere. Way to go, everyone!

The National Bank Virtual Winter Olympics

The Marketing and Acquisitions team at a large, national bank has a big challenge. Just the "M and A" operations are divided into 25 to 40 different offices on any given day, based on employee movement and scheduling, all around the country. How can the company encourage friendships and teamwork among this fragmented workforce? The solution is their FORUM: a twice-yearly challenge.

A recent challenge was Virtual Office Olympics. The clever THEME was perfect, as it complemented the real Olympic games happening at the same time overseas.

The M and A Team's Virtual Office Olympics featured two ACTIVITIES in which teams competed at their locations and used smartphones to video record their challenges (less than one minute long). The first activity was Office Chair Curling, where "office athletes" rolled an empty office chair into a scoring zone, marked on the floor with masking tape. The second activity was the Team Figure Skating Challenge, where teams videoed themselves "figure skating" to their favorite song. All videos were submitted by email.

The event was heartwarming...and a raging success! FOLLOW-UP was natural as employees around the country enjoyed the hilarious videos and learned what different teams considered fun. Kudos to the M and A Team – your brand of fun gets the gold!

The Afternoon 7th Inning Stretch

We work with a large non-profit, who provides a "home away from home" for families of seriously ill or injured children receiving treatment at hospitals around the country. Families can stay together, find some comfort and peace, and enjoy a home-cooked meal after a long day at the hospital.

Working at this organization has its rewards - and challenges. The job can be long and arduous. Many employees live at the facility and are on call 24 hours a day.

Recently, a regional team of managers from several or the regional branches brainstormed ways to add levity to the work environment. They came up with a fun event that could be implemented every day, starting the next day!

The FORUM was the employees' mid-afternoon break. The THEME and ACTIVITY was the 7th Inning Stretch. There are two total teams at each location - Operations and Finance. The operations team would walk through the halls in one direction, while the finance team would walk in the other direction. When the teams crossed paths, they would high five each other. Soon, the activity took on a life of its own, as other staffers joined in and brainstormed ways to enhance the fun.

Let's give high fives to everyone in this organization. They deserve a mid-afternoon break!

Lunch Raps

Ralph, Sabrina, and Rich make up the Employee Health and Wellness Team for a management company that oversees a chain of convenience stores experiencing rapid growth. The Wellness Team promotes health programs and initiatives to help employees stay healthy and save the company millions of dollars over the next 10 to 15 years in health care costs.

The three team members wanted to include some fun into their day. Because they often ate lunch together, their FORUM for fun was lunchtime.

A few times a year, Sabrina, who loves the spoken word and is a serious rapper, creates or freestyles a rap (the ACTIVITY) for Ralph and Rich with a specific theme. One month, the lunch-rap THEME was Wellness.

While Sabrina raps, Rich videotapes the performance on his smartphone. The video is shared later as follow-up to the actual performance.

If you want to know fun, meet Ralph, Sabrina, and Rich from the Wellness Team!

Staff Spring Break at Your College

At a large, private university Pennsylvania, the HR Team

is always searching for opportunities to create fun at work. One spring, they even held a Staff Spring Break.

Staff Spring Break (THEME and ACTIVITY) took place during the students' traditional spring break (FORUM) on campus. After all, why should students have all the fun?

Every day during Staff Spring Break, the HR team offered some fun mini-activities such as arts and crafts, small team challenges, and a luau-themed lunch. Employees were encouraged to take pictures of all the fun. The photos even spawned a "Selfie Challenge" to vote for the staffer with the best Spring Break experience. What a fun follow-up! Who needs Daytona Beach?

Yale Electric Employee of the Month Program

Yale Electric Supply Company is a regional supplier of electrical products and services. Every month, the company presents the Employee of the Month Award to an outstanding employee nominated by coworkers. The award presentation – held as a brief morning ceremony – is a great forum and activity for fun.

Before the event, a direct manager or a close coworker fills out a quick survey about the winner. Survey questions include: Does the employee have interests or hobbies outside of work? Does he or she have any office-approved nicknames? The answers help define the theme of the presentation.

One month's theme, for instance, was the Pittsburgh Steelers, in honor of the award winner, John, an avid Steelers fan. The presentation featured a Steelers-themed trivia challenge. John was even given a "thinking cap" - a cheap, blow-up Steelers helmet! He gladly played along.

Of course, what award ceremony is complete without photos? Every month, pics of the winner are emailed throughout the company (great follow-up).

Yale Electric, you light up the world of engagement!

CHAPTER 8

CREATING YOUR OWN FUN DEPARTMENT

Workplace fun is, well, fun. But it might stress you out a bit when you first get started. Even if you're following our instructions to a T, you might consider yourself the lone pioneer in this new frontier of fun.

You don't want to do it alone, so who will join you in your new Team Fun? You look around the office. Ed is typing furiously on his computer. Susan is engrossed in a client call. Jon is busy fixing a laptop glitch. No one seems remotely interested or available to help you build your own internal fun department.

You're not alone. When we say "you're not alone," we don't mean that others can commiserate. We mean you are l-i-t-e-r-a-l-l-y not alone. That's because:

EVERY ORGANIZATION HAS A FUN DEPARTMENT!

That's right. Every organization we have ever worked with – thousands of them – has had at least a few employees that really know how to bring the fun to any occasion, and they want to do it right now at work. In fact, they already are! Really. You might not recognize the card-carrying members of your new fun club … because you haven't invited them yet or haven't considered their actions as "fun". Believe us, "fun" exists in any organization. Anything, people or user-focused, is "fun". Just imagine rebranding any of the following as "fun";

- HR bringing donuts in to the monthly or weekly meeting

- the Employee Team organizing a chili cook-off

- That "preferred" parking spot in the lot

- A "Thank You" email to co-workers for working extra hours on that project

- Free Coffee and free food of any kind

Yes, "fun" already exists in some form or fashion wherever you work. It just may not be as obvious or apparent as peel and stick letters on an office door. However, if you want to formalize your fun department and get people involved. If you want to reinvigorate that internal employee events or engagement committee, let us give you a few tips on how to manage the process!

RECRUITING FOR TEAM FUN

There are many employees and staff members, typical people you see every day, who want to be official members of your fun department. You just need to ask. And remember – if you don't ask, the answer is always no. That said, sometimes your Team Fun members are employees you'd never expect. They may be long-time staffers who normally keep to themselves; they've just never had the opportunity to lead in some fun. Give them that chance.

(Then again, if you see Susan's, Ed's, and Jon's opportunity to be your fun department as nothing more than a waste of time – or – frivolous or weird or dumb – please do NOT volunteer to be a part of your Team Fun! Let someone else lead the mission. Quit your job. And for everyone's sake, never step foot in another company again!)

As you recruit team members, try to find a cross section of employees who represent 10 to 15% of your workforce. Too often, we see fun departments living solely within leadership or HR. Keep in mind that folks in marketing, operations, and accounting – and even your interns – will have great ideas and lots of zeal. This 10 to 15%, ideally, should be a diverse group. This group should cover different departments and varying levels of leadership.

Then again, give yourself permission to start small. You might not be ready to do a full fun rollout to your entire corporation. You might not be ready to recruit a 10 to 15% cross section. In that case, start with fun in the IT department (after they help Jon fix the copier jam). Or launch some fun with the maintenance crew. Fun is infectious. Other departments will see the fun and will want to follow suit.

Also, you can ask for different types of support. Not everyone in your fun department needs to plan or implement the fun. Instead, some folks can help you champion the cause and encourage their officemates to join in. Most people will enjoy helping you in different ways.

Of course, make sure you recruit an official leader of your fun department! You might volunteer yourself or enlist someone else. You just need someone at the head. If you're the leader – remember, you can't do any of this disingenuously. Don't tell your staff, "Okay, everyone! We'll do THIS for fun because the book said so." Instead, you should enter this exciting, new world of fun with sincerity. If you truly care, your employees will see it, and they'll happily join you.

Finally, as you promote your fun department, keep in mind that it means different things to different people. For leaders, a fun department may be an important business tool to shift or support a culture. For start-up entrepreneurs, it may spark a positive culture from the outset, paving the way to success. For employees, it may represent a meaningful connection to coworkers and a means for happiness and health.

RECOGNIZING THE FUN

In addition, rest assured that you're not completely starting from scratch. Even the littlest bits of fun already exist in your workplace. Look at Betty, who sometimes brings in donuts. Or Peter, who likes giving high fives to coworkers "just because." Or Ed with his fantasy football league. Susan with her lunch meetings. Jon with his copier jams. The question isn't whether there's any fun. It's whether you see it under the official banner of a fun department or something else.

If you already have the resources to buy donuts or give high fives, what leader would say no to similar types of fun?

Fun can exist just about anywhere, with just about anyone, and in just about any form. The trick is recognizing that fun and calling it your fun department.

MEETING AS A FUN DEPARTMENT

Once you formalize your Team Fun, it's time for your first meeting. Are you excited? We are! This is where you'll tap into the awesome brainstorming techniques detailed in Chapter 7. It can be quick. Take no more than 15 minutes for this Exercise: the *FUN FOR ME LISTING EXERCISe*, and another 15 minutes or so to brainstorm

FORUMS, THEMES, ACTIVITIES, and FOLLOW-UP. In just a half hour, some of you should have great ideas ready to roll out. Oh, and give yourself permission to take some risks. You just might like the results.

Meet with the team once per month for 30 minutes as a quick pit stop.

KEEPING THE FUN GOING

Do you wake up every morning and exclaim, "I'm going to have fun at work today!"? Do you hop in the car and grin ear-to-ear because you're commuting alongside thousands of your closest friends on the highway? Wait, they're not grinning either? No kidding!

We get it. Work sucks sometimes. As you roll out your fun department, we don't expect you to flip 180 degrees and become some over-the-top "funster." But as long as you have a sincere desire to help others, you'll have the gumption to keep the fun going.

Constantly build your list of fun ideas. Sure, you'll brainstorm at the monthly Team Fun meetings, but you can also get fresh ideas when you're just hanging with coworkers and have nothing else to talk about. You know those times – at lunchtime when the talk of emails and meetings grows stale or silent; or during that 15-floor, slightly awkward elevator ride with a couple coworkers. In these situations, you can ask some casual-yet-powerful questions to not only break the ice, but also contribute to your fun programming:

- What do you do for fun – at work or outside of work?

- What's been your favorite fun thing we've done at this company?

- *What have you heard, read about or experienced other companies doing for fun?*

- *What did you do for fun last night? Yesterday at work? This past weekend? Past week? Past month? Past year?*

Answers to these questions should give you more ideas for your Creative Inventory.

One more thing, don't be afraid to put fun on the backburner once in a while, if needed. Business changes. Priorities change. If you're experiencing a downturn, focus on paying your employees and meeting their basic needs first. Then again, the sooner you make fun an integral part of your operation, the more you'll contribute to your success and limit those hard times.

So now, get back to work … on your new brand of fun. Find your fun department and make it work for you and your organization. Good luck!

PART III: CONSIDERATIONS

Questions to Consider

- Where is your fun department?

- What do you do every day to ensure your "fun department" shows up?

PART IV

FUN WORKS

CHAPTER 9

OUR ROLE MODELS

So far, we have outlined The Fun Dept.'s model for fun – a program used successfully by thousands of companies. Let's sum up the key components:

- Leadership interest/support/involvement

- Discovering your company's unique brand of fun (which will evolve)

- Identify shared experiences with the Fun For Me Listing Exercise

- Abide by the 3Cs – Consistent, Company Time, and Culture Compliant

- Create fun that appeals to the senses

- Use forums, themes, activities and follow-up to develop your creative inventory

• *Recognize that you already have a fun department, and build from that foundation*

At The Fun Dept., what we love most is seeing the smiling faces of leaders and employees as they use our program and develop an amazing culture of fun. While we've shown you some examples already, let's look closely at a few more success stories. These organizations have done a beautiful job of developing, delivering, and embracing fun. They're role models for us all!

BELFINT, LYONS AND SHUMAN

Belfint, Lyons & Shuman (BLS) is a mid-sized accounting firm with 65 employees. Headquartered in the mid-Atlantic region, BLS serves clients around the world.

The company brought The Fun Dept. into their office in 2009. They were trying to develop an engaged staff and infuse fun into the workplace, but felt they were using a lot of time in the planning phase with little result. What's more, their attempts at fun – the post-work picnic and holiday party – didn't seem to accomplish their objectives: to adapt to a changing demographic in the workforce, boost morale, and break down barriers to knowledge-sharing across the firm. We saw right away that we'd be integrating the 3Cs into the mix, especially consistency and events held on company time. Also in adapting to their changing workforce, they needed events that would cross generations. Many of the partners were getting close to retirement. Younger employees would gradually take over, creating a shift in the workplace environment.

As The Fun Dept. developed a plan to deliver fun throughout the year, we factored in the ebb and flow of their workload. It's an all-hands on deck and high blood pressure frenzy leading up to two major tax deadlines in April and October. Once the deadlines pass, employees' vital signs return to normal. With that in mind, BLS now schedules more fun during the busy season, when employees need fun the most. In fact, BLS has found that fun during the busiest of seasons can be seriously productive.

A typical year of fun for BLS now looks like this:

January

All-staff team event for 90 minutes in the afternoon

February – April

Short, biweekly fun connections and breaks for the team

May – July

Flexible scheduling for fun

August – October

Short, biweekly fun connections and breaks for the team

November – December

Flexible scheduling for fun and promotion of upcoming team event in January

The company also carries out fun in creative ways. For instance, they celebrated their 90th anniversary with a half-hour morning tailgate. (The event was held on April 15th, right after tax season.) As employees arrived at work, team members held up "Congratulations" signs. The tailgate was complete with refreshments and parking lot games like Baggo®. A local radio station was also on site for a live broadcast. Following the event, employees enjoyed seeing photos and videos as souvenirs of their fun.

Other fun events have included tricycle races along hallways in the office, and a mini-golf course set up around the office to provide tournament play.

Since implementing The Fun Dept. model five years ago, BLS has enjoyed consistent boosts in engagement scores, and both the new youth and the experienced managers have connected on all levels. As an added benefit, they're also now attracting a younger, more diverse workforce. And they're consistently recognized as one of the "Top Workplaces™" in their region.

WILMINGTON UNIVERSITY

Wilmington University is a large, regional university with locations in Delaware, New Jersey, and Maryland. Over the last few years, they've enjoyed unprecedented growth; they're one of the fastest growing universities in the nation. The university's 450 employees are spread out over a large area, and some work virtually.

Employee morale and engagement are important to the leaders at Wilmington University. They even created their own fun department (managed by HR) well before ever meeting The Fun Dept.! We were eventually called in because the university faced a growing challenge – indeed, one of growth. As the workforce expanded, employees had fewer opportunities to connect. What started out like the bar at Cheers – where everyone knows your name (albeit without beer) – evolved into an organization with lots of segmented departments and an employee experience focused on workplace health.

Using The Fun Dept. model, Wilmington University now offers a "schedule for fun" that involves staff, faculty, as well as students across as many campuses as possible. The university also holds "sister events" away from main campus as well as virtual fun programming to include everyone:

September
Annual kick-off carnival for faculty, staff, and students

October
**Staff Halloween party and student costume
contests in each class**

November
**Charity food drive coordinated by staff, faculty,
and students across all campuses. Thanksgiving
luncheon for staff and faculty**

December
**Holiday luncheon for staff while students
are on winter break**

January
Staff health fair with student support

February – April
**Short, fun deliveries for the staff around campus,
including video challenges**

June
Themed staff picnic (during the workday over lunch)

July – August
**New student orientation featuring fun scavenger
hunt to encourage students to make their way
aroundcampus and meet staff and faculty**

Wilmington University calls its fun department "The Office

of Positive Mojo." They even give out a monthly Positive Mojo Award to an employee, team, or department that spreads good humor and goodwill throughout the organization. Winners enjoy an awards presentation at their office, recognition on the university website, and an entry into an annual $250 cash drawing!

A noteworthy Positive Mojo winner was the grounds crew, who received countless nominations one February after a major snowstorm. The crew worked rotating 24-hour shifts to clear the parking lots and keep the university open for business. When they were honored at a quarterly update meeting, they got a standing ovation from everyone, including the university president. (We were lucky to attend the meeting and join in the standing "o" – it was incredibly heartwarming!)

Among many other awards, Wilmington University was ranked #19 in Entrepreneur magazine's Best Medium Businesses to Work for 2011. Not bad for spreading some mojo!

VOLUNTARY PROTECTION PROGRAMS PARTICIPANTS' ASSOCIATION, INC. (VPPPA) REGIONAL CONFERENCE

The VPPPA holds national and regional conferences to educate companies on improving their worksite safety and health programs. The subject matter is serious, and sometimes somber. Most conference attendees deal with on-the-job safety incidences and risks of injury.

"Why not lighten up the mood a little?", thought the organizers of one VPPPA regional conference. By injecting fun in small, manageable doses, the organizers could add some levity while still providing the serious education that participants came for.

Working with The Fun Dept., the team came up with this new conference agenda:

Conference Day 1

**15-minute kickoff icebreaker in the morning
two 15-minute breaks featuring fun activities**

Conference Day 2

**Keynote address about a fun, related topic to
"safety" to jumpstart the day and a fun
15-minute activity right after lunch**

Conference Day 3

**15-minute kickoff in the morning with photos
and videos recapping the great experiences
throughout the week**

Conference organizers have seen higher participant morale since implementing The Fun Dept. model. They have also gotten much more positive survey feedback about the information sessions and overall conference takeaways. (It's just like the university health fair discussed in Chapter 6; put some fun into an educational event, and attendees report that they've learned more!)

BLS, Wilmington University, and the VPPPA regional conference are just three of the many wonderful transformations we've seen over the past decade. Do you know a company that's a role model for fun? Please come visit us at www.thefundept.com and tell us about it! Who knows? You just might make it into our next book... or something else fun. We're full of surprises!

CHAPTER 10

WORLD CLASS PRACTICES AND OUTCOMES

In the last chapter, we looked at organizations using The Fun Dept. model with great success. And while we believe we've developed a great model for fun, we also believe there are millions of ways to adapt our model to your workplace. Maybe you want to tip-toe into the world of fun or charge into it full force.

Want to know what "full force" looks like? Look no further than three well-known companies: Google, Zappos.com, and W. L. Gore & Associates. Thanks to their amazingly fun cultures, these companies are shining stars in recruiting, retention, and employee engagement.

GOOGLE – WHISTLE WHILE YOU WORK

"Google's mission is to organize the world's information and make it universally accessible and useful."

This is Google's mission statement, prominently displayed at the top of the company web page. If you didn't already know Google, you'd think they set some crazy, lofty goals. It would take an uncommonly kick-butt team to organize the world's information and make it universally accessible and useful. (We tried it, and we're keeping our day jobs.)

Imagine if Google didn't live up to their mission. Let's say they made it hard for people to access information. People wouldn't "Google" things. They would search Yahoo for answers or "Ask Jeeves".

Fortunately, as we all know, Google succeeds in their mission every day. Their highly creative, motivated team continually invents solutions that benefit the world. And how do they come up with such great ideas? Google is renowned for nurturing a work environment that promotes creativity.

A creative mind is a fresh, well rested mind. Indeed, Google gives employees 20% of any given workday to "do whatever they want." If you work an 8-hour day, 20% of that time – 1 hour and 36 minutes – fits right into our model for fun. Personally, I (Nat) would divide up the time if I worked there. First, I'd take a 36-minute break in the morning. Then, in the afternoon, assuming I had a separate lunch break, I'd take off from 2:00pm to 3:00pm to do something fun. I might walk around campus, work out at the gym, play chess with a coworker, or doodle on some paper! With this schedule, I'd have 3:00pm to 5:00pm to finish my day's work, set up the next day's schedule, and feel refreshed!

Obviously, this model works only when employees take advantage of the time. However, the key here is that Google has made this a policy. It's like saying, "You MUST have fun!" Just like the Seven Dwarfs, employees at Google are required to "whistle while they work!"

ZAPPOS.COM – WEIRD IS GOOD!

The Fun Dept. had the opportunity to interview Tony Hsieh, CEO of Zappos.com. Zappos is an online shoe and clothing shop that's renowned for its culture of fun. And in the company's own words, they "create fun and a little weirdness."

Tony shared that he's extremely protective of his culture. To him, it's more important to hire someone who fits the Zappos culture than to hire someone whose qualifications look good on paper. "We are not afraid to turn down the most highly qualified, smartest, brightest, most creative, Ivy League Ph.D. graduate if they do not fit our culture," says Tony. Above all else, Zappos wants to find people who fit into their culture of fun and a little weirdness.

Weirdness works at Zappos because the people they hire appreciate its value. Trainings and orientations are geared at further cultivating that weirdness. Nothing too weird – just enough to make life more fun for everyone.

What's more, Zappos celebrates their employees' individuality. As Tony described, people work best when they can be themselves. (Of course, this circles back to weirdness, as everyone has a little weirdness within.)

Tony has found that their model of "fun and a little weirdness" leads to better employees and, in turn, better customer service. Overall, it's a smart business model.

W. L. GORE – MAKE MONEY, HAVE FUN

The Fun Dept. works closely with W. L. Gore & Associates, headquartered right in our backyard in Delaware. The company develops and manufactures a wide range of products – everything from electronics to medical devices. They're best known for their GORE-TEX® fabrics.

The single, driving message at W. L. Gore is simple: Make money, and have fun. And they do both. Note that they do not say, "make money and then have fun" or "no fun until money." Instead, the company has built fun into their culture from day one.

But why would W.L. Gore build fun into their culture?

In our years of research, and with help from a few partnered organizations, we have found a correlation to fun and employee engagement.

In fact, we've found a staggering correlation for one specific question, as part of employee engagement surveys: This place is a fun place to work.

Employees that answered yes to this question indicate a 68% correlation to employee engagement. So what does it all mean? In short, if your workplace is fun, people are more engaged, happier, healthier and more productive. Sounds like WL Gore & Associates has this all figured out.

Ok, it's time to wrap-up and put a bow on it.

Remember the romance analogy at the beginning of Chapter 3? This is where you get engaged! Commitment is the first step.

You have removed all the doubt, barriers and red flags. Throughout this book you have learned the value of a fun culture at work as it relates to increased engagement, morale, productivity, wellness, and profitability.

You also now understand the science and methodology of identifying the shared experience for your team, specifically.

As a leader you appreciate the importance of your endorsement and participation.

You've considered our model The Three C's, how to create your fun so it, itself is engaging.

You have identified the Forums, Themes, Activities, and Follow-Up for your own Creative Inventory to take shape.

You may have even identified your internal fun department. Yes, it's there somewhere! Trust us, there are resources within your company who are anxious to get involved.

Now, get out your calendars to schedule your fun. We recommend starting with at least monthly touches. Move to weekly, then daily touches of fun. Continue to allow your fun department to grow and mature until it truly becomes part of your company's culture and fabric of everyday operations.

In the spirit of doing this right and prototyping to perfection, start small with one department or group and work your way towards building a sustainable culture of fun across your entire organization.

Next, think about establishing a measurable baseline so that you can track your results. Imagine the impact of driving your engagement scores higher as a result of creating a culture of fun!

Then, play it forward. Give "fun" to your people and organization. Make your workplace and the world a better place!

Cheers from your friends in Fun,

Nick and Nat

PART IV: CONSIDERATIONS

Questions to Consider

• Aside from the organizations we mentioned, what other companies do you identify as having a fun culture? Do you see enhanced business outcomes as a result?

• Can you make a connection between fun and any of the following outcomes; communication, employee engagement, customer services, employee satisfaction?

• Has your organization ever participated in any company "culture" competition, such as "Top Workplaces™ Program"? Was it beneficial? Did you test fun as a variable, specifically?

ABOUT THE FUN DEPT.®

The Fun Dept., based in the greater Philadelphia Region, has been creating fun in the workplace since 2005. After all, fun makes serious business sense! Our programs range from quick live events to speaking engagements, strategy consultations, trainings, and a line of accredited workshops. (We make a lot of magic happen, and help drive business success, but we mostly live for those moments when we get your CFO to crack a smile - that's when we know we have done our job.)

We hope that, after reading this book, you're excited to create your own fun department. But if you still have questions., if you still want some more guidance and help... if you're asking, "What the fun?"...

Breathe. Simply go to www.thefundept.com and reach out to us. Or call us at (302) 731-8800. Ask about:

- *Scheduling a Create Your Fun Dept. workshop. We'll teach you how to develop your own brand of fun that seamlessly integrates with your company's culture*

• *Checking out* www.thefundeptworkshops.com *to see when our next workshop is coming to your city*

or

• *Hiring us to create, design, and produce your next fun event. Heck, we'll even deliver the fun for you! Plus, we travel. Don't worry – we won't insist on flying first-class. Not that we'd mind, of course.*

If you're really serious about fun at work, ask about having fun for a living. That's right – you can open The Fun Dept. in your area!

Finally, we'd love to hear your success stories. Who knows? You might just make it into the next edition of *Playing it Forward*.

Thank you for reading our book, for embracing our mission, and for spreading our message of workplace fun, for playing it forward.

ABOUT THE AUTHORS

Nat Measley, the CEO and Managing Partner ("Master of Fun") at The Fun Dept., has lived and breathed fun since he was a baby. (Literally. He grew up in chocolate heaven – Hershey, PA!) This Olympic swimmer wannabe and karaoke crooner has two degrees from the University of Delaware – a Bachelor of Science in Sport Management and a Master of Public Administration with a focus on Organizational Leadership. Nat is an experienced public speaker, facilitator, and trainer. He works directly with CEOs, leaders, HR professionals, and administrators to develop fun programming that supports their organizational goals. Nat loves to travel for work, for fun, and oftentimes for both!

Nick Gianoulis is The Fun Dept.'s "Godfather of Fun." He founded The Fun Dept. after seeing the amazing effects of fun while working at United Electric, a company that embraced a "work hard, play hard" culture. Nick brings his rich experience in sales management and operations to support his amazing team at The Fun Dept. Nick encourages his employees to do what they do best … and gets a kick out of seeing the results. Outside of work, Nick gets his fun from sports and exercise; mountain biking is his drug of choice. He also loves traveling around the world and immersing himself in other cultures, creating smiles and laughter along the way. Nick is most proud of his three amazing daughters, close family, and cherished friends.

99

Made in the USA
San Bernardino, CA
13 August 2016